Jeepers

by Craig Rondinone
Illustrated by Tom Simonton

Richard C. Owen Publishers, Inc.
Katonah, New York

When I was little I never had a dog of my own,
but my friends had dogs.

I liked all those dogs, as long as
I didn't have to take care of them.

One day, my mother saw a picture of
a greyhound dog on a poster at the supermarket.
The words on the poster said,

                "I CAN'T RACE ANYMORE.

                    PLEASE SAVE ME."

There was a telephone number to call.

Greyhounds are racing dogs.
They run extremely fast,
but when they don't win races
anymore, their owners get rid of them.
Then these unwanted greyhounds
need good homes.

My mom loves dogs and always wanted one.
After seeing that poster my mom wanted
a greyhound. She called the number,
and the next day she brought home Jeepers.

Jeepers was the skinniest dog I'd ever seen.
He had a muscular body, a deep chest, and long,
thin legs. Mom said that greyhounds are athletes.
They have to be in good shape to race.

Jeepers was three years old when he came
to live with us.

At first I didn't like Jeepers very much.
He was too much work.
He was supposed to be Mom's dog,
but *I* had to take care of him.
Every morning before school and
every afternoon after school,
I had to feed Jeepers and take him out.
I wanted to be with my friends and play sports,
but I had to walk Jeepers.

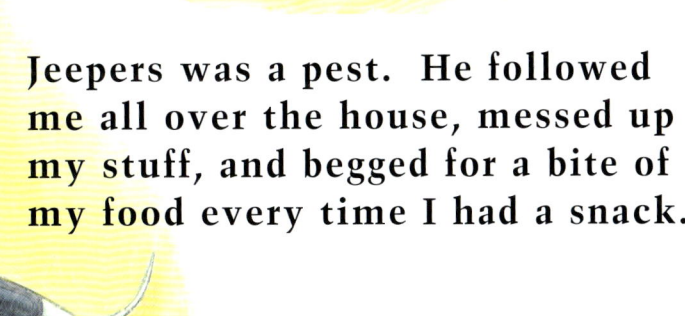

Jeepers was a pest. He followed
me all over the house, messed up
my stuff, and begged for a bite of
my food every time I had a snack.

Whenever I came home from school,
Jeepers was waiting for me. He'd cry with glee
and spin in circles as soon as he saw me.

All I had to say was, "Do you want to go
for a walk?" and he would go crazy. Jeepers loved
to leap and run and be outdoors.

I'd snap on his leash and we'd go out.
Because he was so used to racing, Jeepers dragged me
all over the place. He'd drag me down the street,
right past my friends.

Jeepers was the most popular dog in the neighborhood.
Everyone stopped to say hello to him and pet him.
Jeepers loved the attention and he loved making new
friends. When little kids came up to him he looked
like he was smiling.

But Jeepers was stubborn. When I wanted
to keep walking, Jeepers wanted to stop.
He had to check out every sound and every smell.
When I wanted to stop and be with my friends,
Jeepers wanted to keep walking
and pulled me away.

Jeepers was very strong.
And he could run!

Jeepers could run faster than
any other dog in the neighborhood.
He never got tired. And he could jump real high.

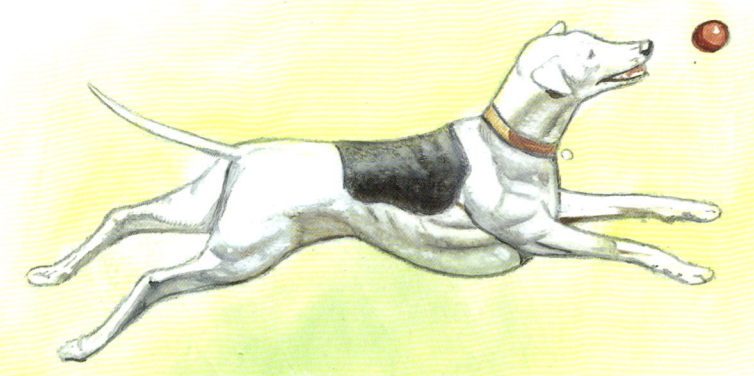

When we played catch, he never missed.
Jeepers was a great athlete. And he was smart.
I taught him to raise his paw and smack
my hand whenever I said, "High five!"

Once Jeepers ran out the front door of our house
and raced down the street. I chased him
for five blocks, barefoot! I only caught up with him
because he sat down to wait for me.

I was so scared he'd run away and I'd never
see him again. I guess I liked Jeepers more than
I thought I did.

He and I were becoming good friends.

Jeepers had never seen stairs until
he came to live with us, and didn't know how
to climb up and down steps.
He'd climb one step, turn around, and go back
to the living room with his head hanging down.

Every time I went upstairs
to my room, Jeepers would whimper
because he couldn't be with me.

I knew Jeepers was smart,
so one afternoon I asked
my friend to come over
with his dog, Lattie.
Lattie knew how to go up
and down stairs.

After watching Lattie do it
a few times, Jeepers tried. Step by step,
slowly and carefully he made his way
up the staircase.

When he reached the top, he looked down at us.
Then—he raced down, made a perfect turn
at the last step, and just missed bashing into
the front door. We all cheered.
Jeepers looked so happy!

Now that Jeepers could climb the stairs,
he slept with me every night.

I think he loved me more than
anyone else in the whole world.

We had become best friends.

But when Jeepers was six, he began to slow down.
He was no longer playful. Years of running races
had made his joints stiff and achy.
That happens to athletes.

Jeepers knew he wasn't like he used to be
and looked really sad all the time.

One night I was reading on my bed, and I heard
Jeepers slowly coming up the stairs. It was so hard
for him to climb them now. He came to my door,
stood there, and looked at me.

Then, he walked to the top of the stairway
and looked back to make sure that I was
watching him.

He stared down at the steps.
Then . . . he leaped up and soared through the air,
stretching his legs out as far as he could.

"Jeepers!" I screamed
as he sailed out and over
the entire staircase.

My mom was downstairs. She heard me scream and saw Jeepers land.

He had cleared the whole staircase in one colossal leap, landing at the bottom and bashing his head against the front door.
The whole house shook!

I rushed downstairs to him.

Jeepers just shook his head,
strolled to his water bowl
for a drink of water,
then looked at us
with a grin on his face.

Mom and I were amazed.
Jeepers was tough.
He was cool.

"I guess he was too stiff
to walk down the stairs,"
Mom said.

"No," I replied,
"I think he always wanted to do that,
and he finally did."

Jeepers had courage. He was fearless and brave.

There are all kinds of athletes—baseball champions, basketball stars, football heroes.
But I think Jeepers was the greatest athlete of all.

Jeepers was my friend.